Introduction

Bonding in terms of fabric may be briefly described as the application of one material to another by means of a fabric glue. It is not only practical and useful but capable of being used to create amazingly subtle or complex surfaces for stitch. Bonding may be used with a huge array of fabrics and is an excellent way of using recycled materials. It was originally sold as a narrow strip of bonding film used to 'stick' hems and turnings in place when heat was applied. There are now many products especially designed to use with fabric and these include 'Wonder Under', fusible web in various forms but most often it is supported on a silicone paper *(Bondaweb)* which can be useful for many of the techniques. There is also a bonding powder which resembles salt in texture and this can be excellent when dealing with small areas and 'tucking in' edges and corners. This product is one which we have both carried on trips abroad and has added to the general embarrassment factor experienced by the embroiderer travelling through customs and immigration with 'unusual items' such as packets of white powder!

There are so many advantages in using bonding film or powder which offer a wealth of creative uses. Some of these are listed below.

• It was always advised to cut simple fabric shapes for appliqué. By ironing *Bondaweb* to the back of a fabric, the paper backing temporarily stiffens it which makes it much easier to cut out intricate shapes. It is particularly helpful when working with very soft, sheer materials which would slip and flop during the cutting action. Once the shapes have been cut out, the backing paper can be peeled away and the motif positioned and ironed to bond in place.

• Bonding fabric shapes to a background cloth eliminates the need to use pins or to tack (baste) in place. This makes it easier to machine the edges if this is the action required.

• Bonding torn or cut pieces of various materials to block in, build up or overlap an arrangement of shapes in a chosen colour scheme quite quickly helps maintain the spontaneity of the work before any additional hand and/or machine stitches are used to define, enrich or add texture.

• It is possible to trap and bond snippets of thread, fabric, glitter and an assortment of tiny fragments, all topped with sheer fabric.

• These methods of bonding make excellent partnerships with a range of mixed media.

Several glues have been developed with fabric in mind but in this book we are dealing with a fusible web or powder. We will be looking at some simple and effective strategies for developing innovative and exciting techniques which not only build applied surfaces but inspire design ideas. We have addressed the use of bonding for practical and decorative items as comprehensively as possible but it should be remembered that these are just the starting points for limitless exploration of this fascinating fabric area. We feel sure that the guidelines, if followed, will ensure successful results and will spur you on to find even more exciting ideas in the future.

Inside cover: Experimental piece inspired by a rock surface. Bonded fabrics, Tyvek, Xpandaprint and textural hand stitches. J.B.

Right: *Sheer fabrics bonded to form a simple but effective pattern. Annette Miller*

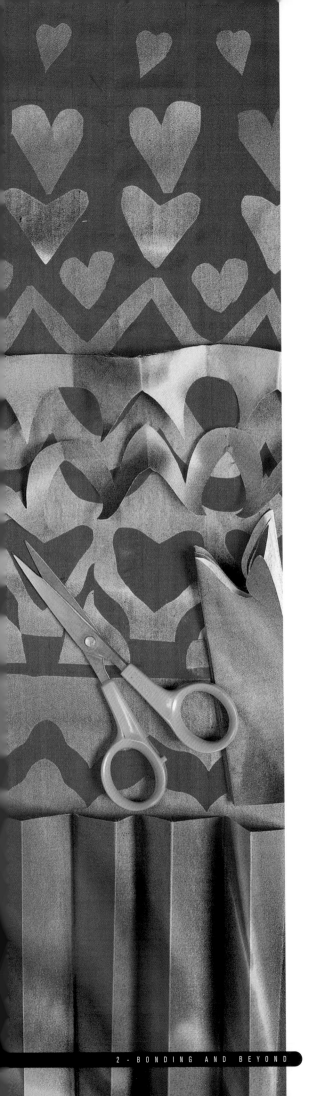

Basic Bonding, 'Cut & Bond' Appliqué

Bondaweb is a versatile and practical material when used for appliqué and there are some useful guidelines which if followed will avoid some of the pitfalls and ensure good results.

• When used with delicate or sheer fabrics *Bondaweb* can alter the surface and render it rigid which may not be appropriate for the desired effect.

• Bonding does stiffen fabric and therefore make it less easy to stitch into. This is not usually a problem and sometimes when machining can be a positive asset.

• If there is a choice, select the appropriate fusible web for the weight and quality of the fabric. There are numerous types on the market.

• Take the function of the item into consideration. A wall hung piece may be treated differently from a practical item where durability, wash and wear may be an important factor.

• *Bondaweb* has the bonus of retarding the fray in frayable fabrics such as velvet and this could be an advantage where the velvet in question may be ironed.

• Bear in mind that this is a glue often supported on a silicone paper for ease of working. When sufficient heat is applied, it melts and care should be taken with the ironing sheet and iron to prevent excess 'glue' making the surfaces sticky and spoiling other fabrics.

Basic Method

• Place sufficient *Bondaweb*, paper side uppermost, onto the fabric and iron using a hot iron until a good bond is made between the fabric and the *fusible web.*

• ALWAYS check the edges. The heat needs to be sufficient to cause the 'glue' to melt and fuse the applied piece to the background fabric.

• ALWAYS check the fabrics first, particularly synthetics to prevent burning or scorching. With delicate fabrics it may be best to overlay with a piece of silicone baking sheet as an extra protection.

• While the backing paper is still attached, draw the shape to be applied and cut it out.

• Place the background fabric right side uppermost on the ironing sheet.

• Peel off the backing from the shape to be applied and place the shape, glue side down, onto the backing.

• Cover the shape with silicone paper for extra protection and iron the shape until a good bond is made.
Depending on the fabrics, manufacturers sometimes recommend for hard wearing qualities that a damp cloth used during the ironing will add strength to the bond.
Even though the bond feels quite secure stitching gives further strength. Many of us will have experienced using a hem bonding strip which did not stay permanent and secure.
Having established the basic technique numerous variations are possible and a few hours spent with some fabrics, *Bondaweb* and an iron and board could produce amazing results.

'Cut & Bond'

The process of cutting and bonding can inspire some wonderful patterns. A simple way to start is by ironing *Bondaweb* onto a strip of fine fabric. Fold the resulting fabric (with the backing paper still attached) into even folds (see illustration).

This is the tricky bit ! Cut out a pattern but leave a part of both folded sides intact or you will end up with separate shapes. Many will have done this as children and made little rows of people holding hands. Most motifs can be adapted to this method with adjustment. Unfold the resulting shape and retain all the off cuts to build up a pattern. Often the 'left overs' form even more interesting arrangements.

When building up a pattern consider contrasts in spaces and shapes.

Think about the basic structure such as diagonal or horizontal and bear that in mind when adding further elements to avoid a muddled effect.

Having bonded the shapes to the background fabric, hand and/or machine stitching may secure and further enhance the design. Sensitive consideration should be given to the tone and quality of threads to enrich and not overwhelm the bonded surface.

Opposite: *A fine hand dyed silk fabric was first ironed onto medium weight Bondaweb before being folded into a concertina. Such a fine silk was made very easy to manipulate in this way because of the firm silicone backing.*
Starting at the bottom, strips of pattern were cut and placed onto a firm silk background.
The shapes were left on paper until the final arrangement was made. In this case the shapes were placed in the order in which they were cut and if pushed back together would form a solid piece of fabric again and this is a simple but effective strategy for forming border patterns.
With delicate fabrics the removal of the paper can be a tricky operation as the fabric can fold back on itself. J.L.

Right: *Using the cut and bond pattern technique described opposite a hand dyed viscose velvet was applied to a silk chiffon. Particular care needs to be taken with thicker fabrics as cutting the 'concertina' can result in more clumsy effects. It is worth the care taken to see the exciting contrast of the thick lustrous patterns on the fine fabric. It also gives the fabric a pleasing weight which hangs well.*
The shapes were machined along the edges of the velvet in a toning thread to secure. J.L.

Bonding & Recycling

This is a wonderful way of using up the tiniest scraps of fabric. Even knitted fabrics may be used effectively with this technique.Very thick fabrics are more difficult to apply as the heat will not penetrate so easily but the bonding will prevent fraying so it also has advantages (and remember that you can turn it over and iron on the reverse to make a better bond).Old silk blouses and household textiles as well as leftover scraps of lurex and crystal etc will be usable with this method.

The throw and cushions pictured right (JL) combine a strong cotton ground with a range of fabric scraps to form a bold and simple pattern.

The bonded fabric shapes were drawn from a range of household textiles such as knitted jumpers (not too thick) velvets, synthetic blends and off cuts from dressmaking and embroidery.

The first stage was to assemble a range of fabrics from which to create the patterns and iron the 'Bondaweb' onto them.

Having decided to base the throw on squares and stripes a range of squares were cut out and placed over the background to form the basic colour balance.The paper backing was left on until the final placing was arrived at. Gradually stripes were added and finally some circles for visual contrast.

When working a large piece like this the most tedious aspect is peeling off the paper backing before ironing to secure.

The cushions were made from the left over squares from the throw and cut into triangles and smaller squares to make compatible but differing cushions. One of the cushions was overprinted with gold silk gutta using a triangular piece of foam sponge.

The machine stitching using a range of matching and contrasting threads was worked to secure the shapes for hard wearing use and with twin needling and zig zag satin stitch to add a further dynamic to the design.

Left: Inspired by the 'tree of life' symbol, this detail from a front section of an elegant coat shows shot fabric shapes bonded to raw silk, machine stitched with details in running stitch. Maxine Cook.

Trapping & Layering

Traditionally it was always advised to cut simple shapes to ease the task of sewing around the edges in order to restrict the fraying. The raw or turned edges were usually stitched in place by buttonhole or herringbone stitches or zig-zag machine stitch, making it extremely difficult to sew neatly around intricate shapes. As already shown, bonding materials enable a greater choice. Tiny snippets of fabric, thread, plastics and glitter can be applied by sandwiching them between the ground cloth and a sheer top fabric. This technique is simple and quick to do but it is not easy to create a subtle beautiful surface without taking time to practice. So often small pieces of material are cut and bonded without regard to integrating them one to another or to the background and the method appears far too obvious. The aim is to convince the viewer to see a sumptuous or intriguing surface allowing the mystery of the creation to be untold.

• Select a background material which may be plain coloured, textured or patterned and should be compatible to the imagery to be created.

• Assemble a range of materials in the chosen colour scheme. Cut, fray and snip fabrics, threads and other substances and place in piles on a tray or in other small containers.

• Gently peel the bonding film from the backing paper. Tear into small pieces and place over the surface to be embellished leaving small gaps between. Cut edges sometimes show if it is not totally fused by heat. Although it would be easier to place larger pieces down the resulting surface could be stiff and not so pleasurable to stitch. The snippets only need to be kept into place until stitchery makes it more permanent.

• Position some of the snippets on top of the bonding film taking great care to distribute the colour and textures to create the desired effect. If a larger area of colour is needed it is often more effective to use tiny fragments rather than one big piece.

Left: Sometimes really sheer fabrics can be difficult to track down. Cheap polyester chiffon scarves available in many colours are the best to use especially if colours and textures bonded beneath need to be prominently featured. If this is not necessary a lesser sheer can be used. In most cases they should be coloured to blend with the background otherwise it could well block out or dull down the subtle arrangement of snippets placed beneath. Transfer fabric paints initially painted on paper are successfully transferred by ironing onto synthetic material. Silk, permanent and metallic fabric paints can also be brushed, sponged or burnished on the top sheer in order to blend it to the background.

A range of curtain and fashion sheers and nets are shown including one placed over a transfer printed cloth. The section which is not coloured is too opaque and dulls the pattern beneath where as the area which has been coloured blends more effectively with the printed image. J.B.

THE BONDING 'SANDWICH'

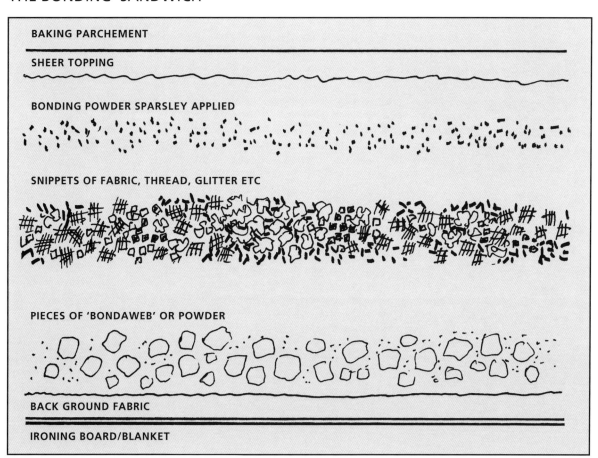

BAKING PARCHEMENT

SHEER TOPPING

BONDING POWDER SPARSLEY APPLIED

SNIPPETS OF FABRIC, THREAD, GLITTER ETC

PIECES OF 'BONDAWEB' OR POWDER

BACK GROUND FABRIC

IRONING BOARD/BLANKET

• Cut edges can look ugly so some fabric pieces should be frayed and partially disintegrated. The rough edges encroaching on each other will help to unify the area. Threads can be pulled from fabrics or snipped into short lengths. Cellophanes, plastics, paper, leaves, petals can all be considered.

• BLEND, INTEGRATE, DRIFT should be words to keep in mind. Tiny snippets of thread or glitter can add finer textures and can be useful aids to linking shapes to one another and to the background.

• If there are too many elements all competing, a 'busy', complicated or fussy surface will result. Select one or two colours or textures that will be reflected throughout and will help to unify the work.

• When all layers are in position, place a few tiny torn pieces of the bonding film on top or sprinkle the bonding powder very sparingly over the area and around the edges.

• Spread over the chiffon or other very sheer fabric, followed by the baking parchment to protect both the fabric surface and the iron. The iron should be set at a moderate heat.

• Iron for a few seconds checking the surface constantly. All traces of the film or powder need to have disappeared but take care not to burn away the sheer top cloth. If this should happen just add a little more bonding medium and a new sheer topping!

Above:
This diagram shows a cross section of the bonded snippets 'sandwich'. The background fabric and sheer topping are the 'slices of bread', the bonding medium the 'butter or margarine' and the snippets form the 'filling'. Remember to use the baking parchment. J.B.

Right:
Inspired by a heavily textured and layered rock surface. Several fabrics and Tyvek were coloured by smudging with metallic fabric paint to give a hint of a glint. The fabric strips were cut with a soldering iron to give an eroded edge and bonded on to the ground fabric. Cross, sorbello, straight and seeding stitches add further textural interest. J.B.

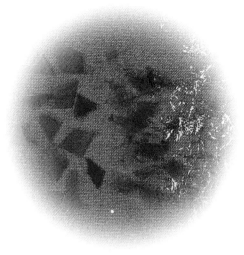

fig 1 - *Cut fragments of cloth blend with each other more effectively if the edges are distressed or frayed otherwise they can be too obvious.*

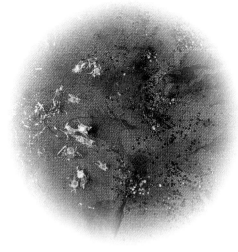

fig 2 - *Sometimes cutting out fabric pieces with a soldering iron gives a more uneven eroded edge.*

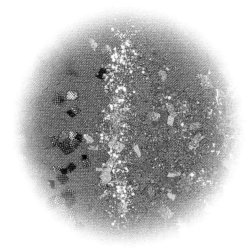

fig 3 - *Tiny snippets of thread, glitter or other particles can help to blend and unify the areas.*

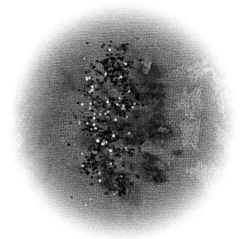

fig 4 - *In order for these materials to be seen clearly the paler colour of the ground fabric used shows too prominently. However the same cloth was used for the piece shown below as many more fragments were layered and integrated. It is really important to spend that little bit of extra time preparing the 'ingredients'. The technique is very easy; to bond a beautiful subtle integrated fabric takes a little more practice. J.B.*

Left: *A piece of 'Peacock Ore' inspired the bonded fabric illustrated. Tiny fragments of fabric, glitter and snippets of thread were bonded under a black chiffon scarf. Machine stitching was worked randomly over the whole piece and a small section shows Sorbello stitch worked in a variety of threads. Care was taken to drift and blend all the elements. An embroidered cloth such as this could be made up as a jacket, a waistcoat, or as a little bag. J.B.*

Mixing Methods

There is no reason why the conventional and freer bonding methods cannot be combined. Ironing the bonding material to the back of the fabric to be applied enables more detailed, accurate shapes and patterns to be cut and positioned. By placing small fragments of cloth or thread on top of bonding film or powder can help link and blend the main shapes and also add texture and subtle colour changes to the whole piece. Generally it is advisable to prepare enough fragments to drift in around and at times encroach the shapes. Some areas can be densely covered, others less so. Be aware of acute tonal changes and allow the coloured snippets being applied to blend in with the background colour. If the spaces showing through are too obvious they may appear busy and spoil the overall unity. Hand or machine stitching can complete the process making a cohesive whole.

• Always remember to be frugal when sprinkling the bonding powder. Too thickly applied it can be difficult to 'melt down'. If used with discretion it is an excellent medium particularly for the final action before applying the sheer fabric topping.

Left: *A transfer painted image printed onto polyester cotton provided the foundation for this design. The flowers were cut from fabric backed with the bonding medium and ironed in place. Small pieces of bonding film and thread snippets were positioned between the flowers to add textural interest and to help integrate the piece. A chiffon scarf was bonded on top to sandwich all the elements. J.B.*

Right: *This piece was backed with piece of felt and machine embroidered to define and unify the whole cloth resulting in a firm, attractive fabric which could be made up into a variety of items. J.B.*

Bonding & Building with Colour

Having established that bonding is an excellent method of building patterns it is also possible to build and layer to create complex and atmospheric designs particularly when using painted *Bondaweb*.

Painted *Bondaweb*

This is a really useful and exciting technique capable of endless variations.

• The *Bondaweb* best used for this technique is a medium weight which comes easily away from it's backing.

• It is possible to use a range of colouring media to colour the *Bondaweb*. Any fabric paints such as silk and permanent which can be applied to fabrics will work as well as acrylic paints. The colouring medium should be capable of being mixed with water as it is this quality which will give some of the most subtle and interesting effects.

• Painted *Bondaweb* may be applied to a range of fabric surfaces from smooth to textured with varying results. The smoother the fabric the more easily it will adhere but the textured results achieved on rougher surfaces will be ideal for interpreting distressed imagery. On paler fabrics the *Bondaweb* patterning is evident but on darker colours a bolder approach is normally called for.

Method

Useful equipment: a piece of foam sponge or similar mixing plate, water pot, old paint brushes.

• Mix the colour on the plate and use water to dilute. The amount of water will dictate the outcome. For a delicate wash of colour, mix with more water and for a more solid look use colour almost undiluted.

• This technique results in a characteristic wrinkling and shrinkage which takes place along the same direction as the manufacturers cut edge. The colour may be applied in a variety of ways and by gently applying it parallel to the edge interesting effects will emerge as the colours dry and the shrinkage occurs. More haphazard and dramatic effects can be achieved by crumpling the *Bondaweb* first. It is also possible to apply the colour in textured and precise ways depending on the required result.

• Allow the paint to dry thoroughly before ironing off.

• Place the painted *Bondaweb* over the ground and iron carefully making sure that the edges are bonded.

• Allow one or two minutes before peeling back the paper backing to reveal the patterns underneath.

The staged samples illustrated here demonstrate the processes involved in completing an intensively worked small panel using various types of bonding.

• Based on an image from Florence, fabrics pre ironed with Bondaweb were cut into a simple pattern and applied. For the purposes of the staged samples the image was repeated four times.

• A piece of painted Bondaweb covering the image was ironed on

• Silver transfoil (a specialist foil designed for use with heat and glue) was placed shiny side uppermost and ironed over the Bondaweb using WOOL setting (no hotter). To achieve a shimmer of silver use the lightest of touch with the iron or it will be completely covered with a solid sheet of silver.

• BEWARE - for this type of foil, which is supported on protective heat resistant plastic, too hot an iron will fuse the metallic surface into the protective sheet and it will not work.

• Even though there is a 'bruising' of silver over the surface there is still sufficient exposed Bondaweb to receive other fabrics and in this case a sheer blue polyester was ironed over the surface thus giving it an interesting blue sheen. (the very finest sheer is to be found in scarves)

• At any point during these processes it is possible to stop but here a further stage has been worked which offers exciting textural possibilities.

• Using a heat tool designed for stamp embossing which resembles an elongated and powerful hair drier a jet of heat was directed at the surface.

• This technique should take place wearing a mask, or outside or in a well ventilated room.

• It works particularly well with sheer nylon or polyester fabrics when the fabric peels back in interesting ways but the bonding retards the peel back and prevents it from disappearing altogether.

• The final step is to stitch and in this case bold tonal hand stitching was first worked before finally machining to produce a richly stitched surface. This technique can be used to good effect when a distressed or muted image is required. The fading splendour of decaying architecture or frescoes etc can be built up and 'knocked back' to achieve an atmospheric interpretation. J.L.

• At first the surface has a slightly sticky feel but it does eventually disappear. If however you wish to cover this surface in an almost invisible way then the very sheerest nylon or polyester scarves may be ironed over to seal, and coloured scarves will add a delicate film of colour to add a new dimension to the play of light on the surface.

Variations

• The painted Bondaweb may be cut or torn into shapes and applied to create a range of imagery.

• Whenever heat is applied it melts again and scraps and fragments may be ironed and bonded to the surface (be sure to place silicone baking sheet over the top to prevent a nasty accident with the iron).

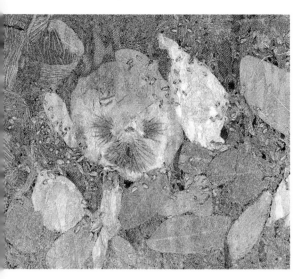

Painted *Bondaweb* has such a range of possibilities that it can become quite addictive. Each time the colours distort on the *Bondaweb* new ideas offer themselves. If the patterning is particularly inspirational then photocopying can preserve it for future reference.

A further development is the trapping of fibres and other materials between two layers of painted *Bondaweb* as in the piece illustrated above. (JL)

To achieve the delicate lace like structure take a piece of painted *Bondaweb* large enough to be folded in two. It must be dry for the best effects.

• Place the painted *Bondaweb* with backing intact and painted side uppermost on the ironing sheet and on one side only place the materials to be trapped. In this case there are dried flowers and leaves as well as some fibre and glitter.

All sorts of fabrics and fibres may be used depending on the desired effect. Care should be taken with the positioning as it is all too easy to end up with an uncoordinated messy texture.

• Fold the *Bondaweb* carefully into a 'sandwich' so as not to disturb the arrangement.

• Place a piece of silicone paper over the whole piece and iron with a hot iron until the two halves are fused.

• Wait a few moments as this helps the peeling back. Gently prize the two layers apart by removing first one side and then the other. This is a delicate operation but the results are worthwhile.

• Next take two pieces of sheer nylon or polyester and place the bonded texture between them. Make sure there is silicone baking sheet protecting underneath and above the piece.

The very sheerest nylon scarves are the only ones which offer the lacy possibilities and it can be effective to combine colours and have a contrast on the top and bottom as in this piece.

• The nylon sheers adhere to the *Bondaweb* with a firm bond and make a tough but lacy fabric. It is also possible to make holes by using the heat tool (sadly a hair drier does not work in the same way). The bonding retards the heat where there is a firm bond but there are little pockets of air where the trapped materials occur and it is here that the sheer fabric peels back to make lacy organic holes.

Right: This piece entitled 'Postcard from Kitchener' is one of a series of postcards based on a wonderful visit to Canada in the snow.

On a base of neutral coloured linen a range of fabrics was cut and bonded to describe some of the imagery and experiences of the trip. There is a log cabin feel to the piece as I actually stayed in a traditional log cabin and the hearts are derived from a gallery I visited which was full of pieces of work based on this motif. When I had composed the shapes I did not feel the piece truly represented the atmosphere of Canada in the snow and covering it with delicately painted Bondaweb achieved the desired effect. Finally a layer of sheerest polyester chiffon was ironed over to seal the surface before some hand and machine stitching to add points of emphasis. J.L.

Left: It is possible to cut or tear different coloured Bondaweb's into patterns or images.

The tiles here were cut from painted Bondaweb and ironed into overlapping patterns before delicate squares of sheer polyesters were applied to add further transparent layers. J.L.

Bonded Beads & Brooches

Many embroiderers continue to be fascinated by beads and the huge variety now available to buy is very tempting. Paper, wire and the bead modelling materials offer a further range. However, intriguing customised beads can be made by bonding fabric together. There are certain projects where conventional beads look too obvious whereas ones made from cloth may be more sympathetic to the surface being created.

• Iron the bonding adhesive to the back of the fabric initially leaving the backing paper in place to ease the cutting process especially if the materials are soft or sheer.

• After paper trials to determine scale, cut the fabric to the required width or length. Blunt or tapered ends give different results.

• Peel the backing paper away. Roll the fabric around a 'core' rod such as a length of fine dowling, wire, a kebab stick or the handle of a paint brush. The diameter of the rod chosen dictates the size of the hole needed for sewing or threading through.

• Temporarily secure the fabric in place with a short length of fine wire to prevent the material from unfurling, or hold in your fingers until placed under a sheet of baking parchment and ironed in place. Gently roll the 'core' stick to ensure the heat has activated the bonding material throughout and fused the layers of cloth together evenly to form a secure shape.

• Untwist the wire unless it is left in place as a decorative feature.

• Remove the bead from the rod. Applying talcum powder on the core rod before making the bead will eliminate any slight sticking on its removal.

• Remember to use baking parchment on the ironing surface for protection as well as between the iron and the bead.

• An alternative method is to fuse the layers together with a hot tool. Extreme care needs to be observed as fabrics can be burnt in prolonged heat. If eroded, organic or antique effects are required, this method could be useful. Always allow time to practice first before embarking on a piece of work.

• Roll the fabric backed with bonding adhesive around the 'core' rod as before and fix in place with a small wire. Making sure that your fingers are well away from the heat, twizzle the stick in front of the heat gun carefully observing the fusion and slight disintegration. Leave to cool before removing the 'bead' from the rod.

• Most synthetic fabrics will fuse together without a bonding agent where as natural fibres will burn and not bond together unless it is included.

• As you can see from the photograph, a wonderful assortment of fabric beads can be created to enrich the colour and textural qualities within your work. Additional wrapping, beading or wiring can embellish them further if appropriate. J.B.

Beads & Brooches

This array of brooches and beads have been created with a combination of the methods already described in this book.

The brooches are made from a stiff pelmet *Vilene*. Each brooch has a base of two pieces for thickness which have been first painted with either acrylic or silk paints before being enriched with further bonded shapes or covered with painted *Bondaweb* and foil for the metallic look.

Some have been further covered with polyester sheer chiffon and the heat tool used to distress.

On some brooches a synthetic velvet has been covered with painted *Bondaweb* and foiled before incising with a fine soldering tool to achieve the delicate indentations. In this way it is possible to arrive at an interesting metallic effect whilst still maintaining some textile properties.

The textured organic shapes are coloured fine *Tyvek* fibre to which metallic burnishing cream has been added before ironing into 'filligree' shapes.

The fabric beads have also been made from synthetic velvet which was covered with painted *Bondaweb* and foil before being cut into long triangular shapes and wound round a fine wooden 'kebab' stick for ease of working. The soldering tool has been used to fuse the beads together and deep incised marks burnt through the layers to form chunky 'ethnic' looking beads. J.L.

Mixed Media Bonding

Intriguing effects can be achieved by bonding snippets of fabric and thread onto *Tyvek* (also named fibre film). Before progressing to this technique you need to discover the potential of this material. It is a fascinating medium and can be purchased in various forms; as a fibrous sheet of paper in varying thickness or as a thin crinkly 'fabric'. It is usually white although a small range of colours is now available. This unique material is used on building sites, for kites, protective clothing, banners, legal documents and envelopes amongst other things. Being extremely durable it does not tear and is not destroyed by water. However it does disintegrate to form organic or lacy surfaces when heat is applied by iron or hot gun. If it is not integrated sympathetically with the technique or the stitching it is partnered with, it can look far too obvious and gimmicky. *Tyvek* can be coloured, stitched and have other materials bonded to it, offering other interesting surfaces to consider.

Before combining with bonded appliqué, practice cutting pieces of *Tyvek* and applying heat to it by iron. Always use baking parchment or a silicone sheet between the iron and the medium to protect the surfaces. Experimentation will give you some experience towards sensing and knowing how much and for how long heat should be applied in order to gain certain results. Making cuts with scissors or a soldering iron into the edges and within the piece give different effects. Any incision weakens the material and it therefore reacts to the heat more quickly.

This material can be coloured with wax crayons, thin applications of acrylic or fabric paint and other colouring media. The colour can be sponged, printed or smudged on to obtain the required look. A thick layer of paint, bonded appliqué or stitchery can lessen or control the effect of the heat so that the distortion and disintegration is not so speedy. Remember to colour both sides as when the heat is applied the underside may crinkle and fold into view allowing the white to intrude or spoil your design.

- Colour the *Tyvek* on both sides in the chosen colour scheme and allow to dry.

- Consider whether to incise the material by cutting with scissors or soldering iron. This would be the right action if an uneven eroded effect is wanted.

- Tear the bonding material into pieces and place on top. Do not worry about overlapping the edges.

- Place tiny pieces of cut and distressed fabric or small snippets of thread, plastic etc. Sprinkle a little bonding powder on top.

- Cover with the sheer fabric and baking parchment for protection. Gently but firmly iron the surface taking time to observe whether the additional materials are bonded.

- Take care to apply the heat in different directions. Heavy handed flat ironing will not allow areas to rise up and become slightly dimensional. Applying heat carefully with a hot gun may be advantageous.

- After the first ironing, the pieces may have adhered but the *Tyvek* may not have shrunk or distorted as required. Turn the piece over not forgetting the sheets of baking parchment to protect the ironing surface and the iron and apply more heat. Take care not to iron the medium totally away. You can often observe the rapid process through the baking parchment but not so easily through a silicone sheet.

- It may take a little practice before creating a dimensional decorated surface that you like. On doing so it can then be stitched and incorporated within a piece of work.

Right:
Tyvek *fabric coloured with silver paint.*

fig 1 - *Shows incisions made with a finely pointed soldering iron*

fig 2 - *An incised piece having been heated by an iron or heat gun. Note the shrinkage.*

fig 3 - *Snippets of fabric, thread and glitter topped with chiffon was bonded to the* Tyvek *resulting in a subtle, dimensional surface.*

fig 4 - *A similar section shown integrated within a larger piece and before any stitching was worked to complete the unifying process. J.B.*

Bonding adhesives can feature within a number of techniques, some of which have been mentioned previously such as making beads, using hand and machine stitching and *Tyvek* worked alongside bonded appliqué. Partnering various techniques or including mixed media present fascinating challenges and may suggest exciting methods to consider extending in the work process. The following suggestions offer intriguing possibilities.

• Shadow quilting offers an alternative technique. This is a method where strongly coloured shapes are trapped between two layers of transparent material (traditionally white organdy). Patterns can be bonded in place before being permanently stitched in position through both layers. A pale semi-opaque fabric such as organdy allows the brightly coloured images beneath to show through in a shadowy way. Although the bonding process makes this method easier to tackle, some embroiderers prefer the undulating effect of the fabric set between the layers and not flatly adhered. It is a case of personal preference.

• As already stated attractive, individual lengths of cloth can be created by bonding fabric shapes to a background material and decorating them further with hand, machine or beaded embroidery before cutting out and making up into a jacket, waistcoat, cushion or bag.

• This unique fabric can be incorporated in all types of patchwork, perhaps hexagons pieced together or exquisitely decorated and placed as the central sections within log cabin or cathedral window techniques.

• Attractive lacy patterns can be made by pulling and re-arranging the threads of loosely woven fabrics or scrim. These can be further embellished by bonding two sheer fabrics together, sandwiching the pulled fabric between. Trapping other materials within the sheers can offer other innovative avenues to explore. Strips of bonded cloth could also be darned through an open weave material affording other experimental opportunities.

• Sheets of fine expandable modelling wire mesh is another medium to consider.
Wire Form now available in art shops can be cut, shaped, moulded, gathered and wrapped for all sorts of art and craft work. The mesh can be sandwiched and bonded between two fabrics, the top having been bonded, stitched and decorated as required beforehand. It is also possible to add further stitching or decorative effects when the 'sandwich' has been constructed and before manipulating the wired fabric into an unusual surface. After experimentation a number of exciting dimensional projects could materialise. Alternatively smaller raised areas could be set in a piece of textile work if an organic type of surface is envisaged.

Left: A Lichen textured tree bark inspired this experimental sample where a wire mesh was bonded between the decorated top surface and the backing cloth. Knots and variations of straight stitches were worked through all the surfaces before the piece was manipulated into an arrangement of ridges. J.B.

Right: This sample was inspired by an interesting rock surface where smooth areas contrasted with crevices filled with small stones and weed. The flat sections of fabric were bonded in the conventional manner (see page 2) and the textured ones with fabric and thread snippets under chiffon with bonded Tyvek and fabric beads sewn on top. Machine and hand stitches added further embellishments. J.B.

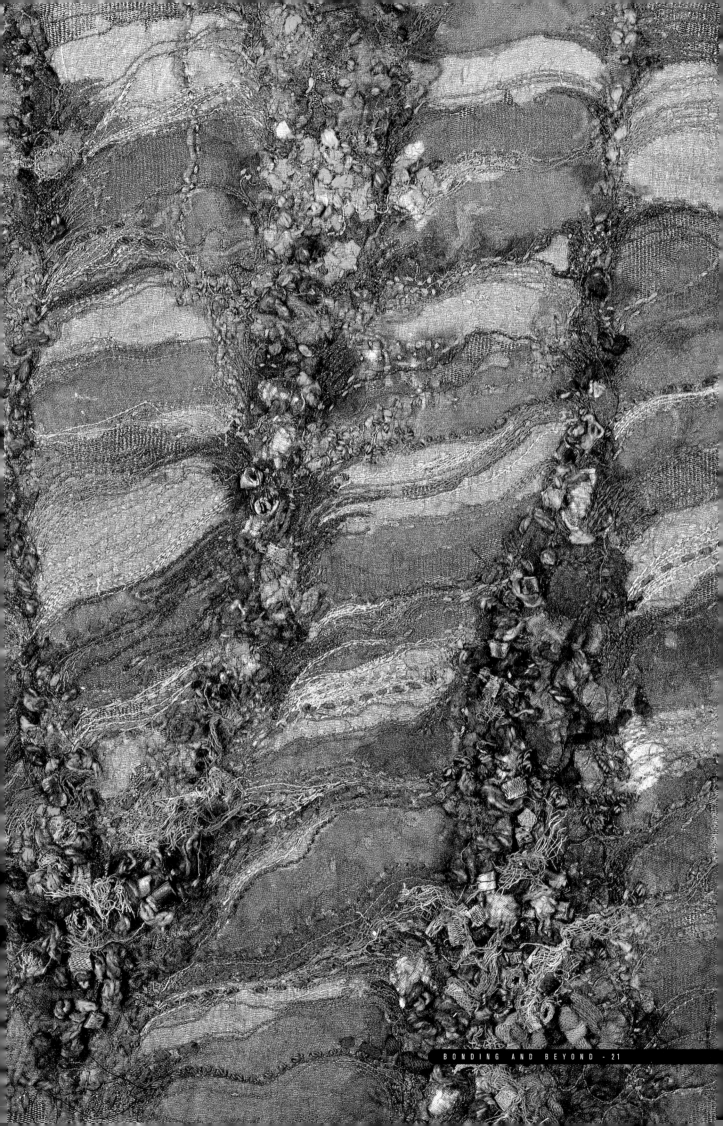

Conclusion

By combining the various techniques already described in the book the possibilities are endless. As we often emphasise, anything which is utilised merely because it is the latest trend or a gimmick is worthless unless it is used with discretion and purpose. Layering and texturing of different types of bonding offers the possibility of a huge variety of surfaces and these can be combined with further texturing mediums where appropriate. The versatility of bonding becomes apparent as soon as you stand at the ironing table with some *Bondaweb*, fabrics, and an iron.

It can be bold, angular and practical as well as delicate, ephemeral and atmospheric. Bonding may be incorporated into clothes and functional household items and used to promote expressive imagery for wall hung work.

We have spent hours exploring these techniques and not every piece succeeded but the more we worked the more interesting it became.

We would recommend working notebooks with samples and simple notes as a good way of recording techniques.

Our aim was to offer the results of a great deal of experience and help readers to avoid some of the problem areas but we both believe that our suggestions should be looked on as starting points and fully expect that armed with this information you can achieve your own exciting work.

Right: Grey
Work in progress. This piece of work from the 'Touch Wood' series celebrates the patterns in trees combined with some references to superstition, myths and legends.

The background is synthetic velvet with coloured Bondaweb applied followed by a delicate shimmer of silver foiling.

Onto this ground, coils of torn, twisted wrapped fibres were bonded (with great difficulty) just sufficiently to hold them in position for ease of working.

Over the top of this another layer of painted Bondaweb was ironed and again foiled with a layer of polyester chiffon applied over the entire surface.

The last operation was to use the heat tool to 'zap' away the Bondaweb and chiffon in the gaps and crevices to produce a semi organic form ready for stitching. J.L.

Left: Touch wood - Angry Sun
On a base worked in a similar way to the grey piece, hand stitch has been worked using thick silk threads in an organic rhythm appropriate to the image.

This piece celebrates the powerful noonday sun in the heat of a Turkish Island.

It also refers to the fierce heat and the fact that there was a ram tethered to a tree in the full glare of the sun and it was due for ritual slaughter as a good luck symbol. The ram's horn forms a strong element in the imagery. J.L.

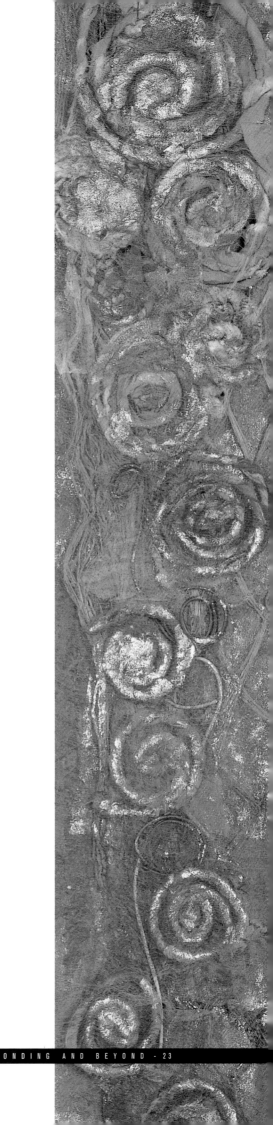

Suppliers

General Art Supplies, Transfoil etc

Art Van Go
16 Hollybush Lane,
Datchworth, Knebworth,
Herts. SG3 6RE
Tel: 01438 814946

Gillsew
Boundary House,
Moor Common,
Lane End, High Wycombe,
Bucks. HP14 3HR
Tel. 01494 881886

George Weil & Sons Ltd
The Warehouse
Reading Arch Road,
Redhill, Surrey. RH1 1HG
Tel: 01737 778868

The World of Embroidery
always contains a range of
excellent suppliers.
Apt 41 Hampton Court Palace
East Molesey. KT8 9BB
Tel :0181 943 1229

Bondaweb
may be bought at Department
Stores such as John Lewis.

Strata
Oronsay, Misbourne Avenue,
Chalfont St Peter,
Bucks. SL9 Tel.01494 873850
Tyvek (Fibre film)

Fashion 'N' Foil Magic
PO Box 3746,
London. N2 9DE
Tel : 0181 444 1992

Whaleys (Bradford Ltd.)
Harris Court,
Great Horton,
Bradford,
West Yorkshire.
BD7 4EQ
Tel:01274 576718

Supermend
P.O. Box 300, Basildon,
Essex. SS14 3RT
Tel. 01268 271244

L&B Embroidery
28 Leigh Road,
Andover,
Hants. SP10 2AP
Tel: 01264 365102
Soldering Iron

Inca Studio Ltd
10 Duke Street,
Princes Risborough,
Bucks. HP27 0AT
Tel: 01844 343343

Angela Ramsay
Fron Isaf
Llanglydwen,Hebron,
Whitland, Carms.
SA34 OJX Wales
Tel. 01994 419523
Silk,wool and paper fibres for
bonding

Quilters' Resource Inc.
Double Trouble & Textile
publications,USA
PO BOX 148850,
Chicago, IL60614.
Tel.(001) 773 278 5695

Further Reading
Vanishing Act, Bk-1 - Jan Beaney.
Double Trouble Enterprises.

Voluptuous Velvet, Bk-2
- Jean Littlejohn.
Double Trouble Enterprises.

Transfer to Transform, Bk-4
- Jan Beaney & Jean Littlejohn.
Double Trouble Enterprises.

Stitch Magic - Jan Beaney, Jean
Littlejohn, B.T.Batsford 1998

A Complete Guide to
Creative Embroidery -
Jan Beaney, Jean Littlejohn,
reprinted B.T.Batsford 1997

The Art of the Needle,
Century, London 1988

The Complex Cloth - Jane
Dunwold, Fiber Studio Press 1996

Acknowledgements
Our thanks go as always to our
husbands Philip Littlejohn and
Steve Udall for their generous
help and support and to
Victoria Udall for her typing
skills at late hours.
We would also like to thank
Michael Wicks for the
photography and Jason
Horsburgh for the design &
production of the book.
Printed by Gemini Press Ltd.

Inside back cover:
Byzantine Mosaic (detail)
On a background of synthetic velvet
layers of further velvets, hand made
paper and knotted fabrics have
been layered up and covered with
painted Bondaweb.
A sheer chiffon scarf was bonded
over the whole image before being
burnt back with a heat tool and
marks etched in with a soldering
tool. Hand stitching completed the
texture. J.L.